Ways to Organize
Your **Life**

Deborah Underwood

www.raintreepublishers.co.uk
Visit our website to find out
more information about
Raintree books.

To order:
☎ Phone 0845 6044371
📄 Fax +44 (0) 1865 312263
✉ Email myorders@raintreepublishers.co.uk

Customers from outside the UK please telephone +44 1865 312262

Raintree is an imprint of Capstone Global Library
Limited, a company incorporated in England and Wales
having its registered office at 7 Pilgrim Street, London,
EC4V 6LB – Registered company number: 6695582

Text © Capstone Global Library Limited 2011
First published in hardback in 2011
Paperback edition first published in 2012
The moral rights of the proprietor have been asserted.

Edited by Andrew Farrow and Vaarunika Dharmapala
Designed by Richard Parker
Picture research by Ruth Blair
Originated by Capstone Global Library Ltd
Printed and bound in China by South China Printing
 Company Ltd

ISBN 978 1 406 21749 0 (hardback)
15 14 13 12 11
10 9 8 7 6 5 4 3 2 1

ISBN 978 1 406 21779 7 (paperback)
16 15 14 13 12
10 9 8 7 6 5 4 3 2 1

British Library Cataloguing in Publication Data
Underwood, Deborah.
101 ways to organize your life.
646.7-dc22
A full catalogue record for this book is available
from the British Library.

Acknowledgments
We would like to thank the following for permission to
reproduce photographs: Alamy p 48 (Image Source);
pp 4 (John Lund/Blend Images), 6 (Heide Benser),
17 (Latin Stock Collection), 18 (Ursula Klawitter),
21 (Tim Pannell), 22 (Image Source), 29 (Emma
Shervington), 30 (Image Source), 41 (Amanda Lynn/
First Light), 45 (Dex Images), 46 (Randy Faris), 51
(Estelle Klawitter); iStockphoto pp 10 (Silvia Jansen), 20
(Nikola Hristovski), 23 (aguirre_mar), 32 (atlasphoto),
35 (Peeter Viisimaa), 42 (Andy Dean), 44 (Ola
Dusegård), Photolibrary pp 8 (Photononstop/Hervé DE
GUELTZL), 19 (Polka Dot Images), 27 (Rubberball/
Jessica Peterson), 34 (Corbis InsideOutPix), 37, 38
(Blend Images), 40 (Oredia/Boutet Jean-Pierre);
Shutterstock pp 7 (Poleze), 13 (Natalia Siverina), 15
(Franck Boston), 24 (Benis Arapovic), 26 (peresanz), 28
(Yuri Arcurs), 33 (HomeStudio), 36 (HomeStudio), 39
(Khomulo Anna), 43 (Thomas Owen Jenkins).

Cover photograph of a teenage girl text messaging
on her mobile phone reproduced with permission of
Corbis (Patterson Graham/Blend Images).

Every effort has been made to contact copyright holders
of material reproduced in this book. Any omissions will
be rectified in subsequent printings if notice is given to
the publisher.

Disclaimer
All the internet addresses (URLs) given in this book
were valid at the time of going to press. However, due to
the dynamic nature of the internet, some addresses may
have changed, or sites may have changed or ceased to
exist since publication. While the author and publisher
regret any inconvenience this may cause readers, no
responsibility for any such changes can be accepted by
either the author or the publisher.

Contents

This book belongs to Waltham Forest Libraries

In order to protect the privacy of individuals featured in case studies, some names have been changed.

Words appearing in the text in bold, **like this**, are explained in the Glossary.

Why should I want to get organized?

Have you ever missed an event because you lost your ticket or arrived late? Have you panicked because you couldn't find something your best friend lent you? Have you ever got bad marks because you didn't leave enough time to do your homework? If so, it's time to get organized!

How do you want to spend your time?

If you think organization is deadly dull, don't worry – it's not! The point of organization isn't to have the tidiest room in the world. Being organized allows you to free up your time and energy for the things you want to do.

Write a list of your five favourite things to do. These could be playing music, hanging out with your friends, dancing, writing, paint-balling, or even sleeping. No matter what activities are listed, getting organized will give you more time to do them. This book will help you. So let's get going!

If you get organized you can spend your time doing what you love instead of searching for your socks!

Quiz

How organized are you?

1. You've got to hand in an English assignment tomorrow. How's it going?
   - a. It's been in my "completed assignments" folder for the last three days.
   - b. I'm just checking it over for typos, but should have it finished in plenty of time.
   - c. Er – I've got an English assignment due in *tomorrow*…?

2. You're going to a concert with your best friend this weekend. Where are the tickets?
   - a. They're stuck to my pinboard, along with directions to the venue.
   - b. I'm pretty sure they're in my desk drawer.
   - c. Uh – hang about… *I* was supposed to get the tickets…?

3. A newspaper reporter is taking photos at your school today. You want to wear your favourite shirt. Where is it?
   - a. It's cleaned, ironed, and hanging on my wardrobe door.
   - b. It's in the laundry basket, but I'll wash it tonight.
   - c. I think it's in the pile at the bottom of my cupboard.

Find out the truth!

If your answers are:

Mostly a's: good work. You're already very organized, but you'll still find some good tips here.

Mostly b's: not bad – but there's still room for improvement.

Mostly c's: you definitely need help. But fear not, help has arrived! Turn the page, and turn your disorganized life around!

Organizing basics

Following some simple organizing rules will make your job much easier. Here are a few to get you started:

01 Everything needs a home. This may be the most important organizing rule ever! If you know where your stapler is supposed to go, it's easy to put it away and to find it again.

02 Keep similar things together. Keep all your football gear together. Store your cosmetics in one place, not scattered all over the house.

03 Set a timer. If your whole room is a wreck, it may freak you out if you try to tackle it all at once. Try doing just 20 minutes at a time. You'll be amazed at how much progress you can make.

04 Clear up visible areas first. It's brilliant to spend an hour organizing your sock drawer. But when you've finished and shut the drawer, the top of your chest-of-drawers will look the same. So tackle the bits you can see first. When you see how great it looks when it's all cleared up, you'll be motivated to keep going!

05 Take "before" and "after" photos. It can be satisfying to see how much progress you've made.

06 A shelf of blank boxes isn't very helpful! If you box things up, label the outsides of the boxes.

If you label the outside of your storage boxes, you'll be able to find things more easily.

Q Why should I get organized? I don't care if I'm surrounded by mess!

A Everyone's different, but lots of people find that more mess equals more stress. If you're one of them, clearing out some clutter will make you happier. That's one very good reason to clear up!

If you're still not sure, try this exercise. (You need to close your eyes for it, so read it first!)

- Find a quiet place where you won't be interrupted. Sit quietly with your eyes closed.
- Picture a cluttered part of your life, such as your room or your rucksack. See it in your mind. Can you feel any tension in your body? Is your breathing deep or shallow? Do you feel happy or stressed?
- Now picture the same area neat and tidy without the mess. Do you feel any changes in your body? Do you feel more tense or more relaxed? What's your breathing like?

Take a "before" photo of your room when it's messy. Then take an "after" shot once you've cleaned it. Pin the photos on a notice board to remind yourself how much nicer it is when it's tidy and organized.

07 Work on one area at a time. If you just do a little bit here and there, you won't see progress as quickly.

08 Use a system that works for you. It doesn't matter if no one else understands it. If it makes sense to you to store your underwear and umbrellas in the same drawer because they both start with a "u", fine!

09 Store things near where you use them. If you practise bagpipes in your bedroom, that's where your music and music stand should live, too.

10 Break big jobs down. You may not have time to clean your whole desk, but what about doing a single drawer?

11 Keep containers nearby when you're de-cluttering. When you're sorting out your clothes, you might have one container for things you want to donate to charity, one for worn clothes to throw away, and one for clothes that need repairing. When you're sorting paper, the categories might be "recycle", "file", and "take to school".

12 Let an adult take a look at things before you get rid of them. Your mum might know someone who can use your outgrown clothes, for example. Or your dad might want your battery-operated T-rex for himself!

No time to clean your whole room? Do one job – such as vacuuming – and save the rest for later.

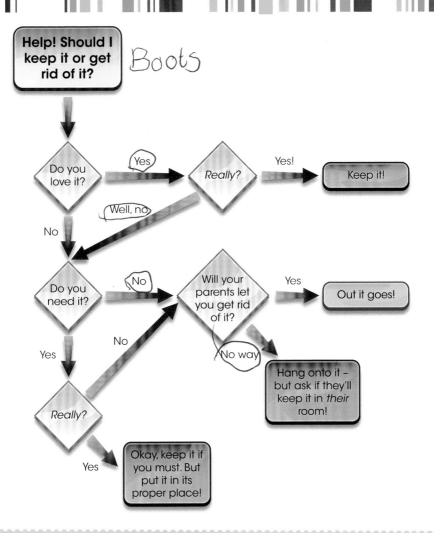

Help! Should I keep it or get rid of it?

Boots

Do you love it? —Yes→ Really? —Yes!→ **Keep it!**

Do you love it? —No↓

Really? —Well, no↓

Do you need it? —No→ Will your parents let you get rid of it? —Yes→ **Out it goes!**

Do you need it? —Yes↓

Will your parents let you get rid of it? —No way→ **Hang onto it – but ask if they'll keep it in *their* room!**

Really? —No↗

Really? —Yes→ **Okay, keep it if you must. But put it in its proper place!**

Q But I'm a creative person! Won't getting organized ruin my creativity?

A No, no, and no! Unfortunately, lots of us have the idea that creative geniuses thrive on mess. Not true! Are you a painter? Think of how many more paintings you'd produce if you weren't stuck with ruined brushes you forgot to wash. Do you make jewellery? You'd make a lot more if you weren't searching through boxes for those beads you bought last summer. Do you write? You'd write more if you weren't hunting for your notebook in your desk, your locker, the car, the fridge (well, it's got to be *somewhere*…).

Organize your school stuff

We all know it's important to do as well as you can in school. Some people act as if they don't care about getting good marks, but deep down they do. No one wants to do badly or have teachers nagging at them all the time. Who do you think looks cooler: the person who doesn't try and gets rubbish marks, or the person who has things under control?

If you want to do your work properly, but as quickly as possible, it's time to organize your study space, your lesson notes, and your thoughts.

It's hard to find what you need in a huge stack of paper! Keep your class notes in binders or files for easy access.

BE SMART

Got a problem? Find a solution that works for you. If you hate ring binders, use spiral notepads instead. If your handwriting looks like a toddler's scribble, type your notes on a computer to make studying easier. Spend a little time thinking about what's working for you now and what isn't. A few small changes can make a big difference!

What's going on now?

Have you ever run out of paper when you were trying to print an assignment? Is your rucksack full of old paper you don't need? When you need to revise for a test, can you find your lesson notes?

13 Make a special study area where you keep everything you need for your homework: paper, pens, stapler, notepad, and folders.

14 Make sure you have a good desk lamp so you don't strain your eyes.

15 "Oops – it's 1.00 a.m., my assignment is due in tomorrow, and I can't print it out because I've run out of paper." Don't let this happen to you! Keep an extra stash of paper and printer ink.

16 Put homework in your rucksack as soon as you finish it. You may have written the most brilliant essay ever, but if the teacher asks for it and it's on your desk at home, it's not going to do you any good.

17 Yikes! Two assignments due on the same day! But as long as you know ahead of time, it's no problem. Write due dates on a calendar so you always know what deadlines are coming up.

 My desk is the dining-room table. How am I supposed to organize my study space?

 If your usual study spot is outside your bedroom, get a basket or box for the supplies you need. You can carry it back and forth, or find a spot nearby to tuck it away. This will keep things together, save you trips back to your room, and make for easier clear-up when tea's ready.

A shipshape rucksack

What's in your rucksack? Books? Dirty PE clothes? Old sweet wrappers? The bit of work you were supposed to hand in last week, now decorated with orange juice stains and ink from a leaky pen?

Your rucksack is like your portable office. Use it wisely and it will make your life easier. Let it get out of control and it's just one more mess to deal with. If your rucksack is full of crumpled paper and mysterious mouldy food items, it's time for a clear-out.

18 Take everything out. You might want to do this on your bed so you can spread things out and see what's there. (Make your bed first!)

19 Clean out any stray bits of paper, paper clips, apple cores, and food crumbs. Turn your rucksack upside down over a waste bin and shake it. If the inside is really disgusting, you may need to wipe it out with a damp cloth. (Make sure the inside is dry before you repack it.)

20 Now look at what was in your rucksack. Were you dragging things around that you don't need? Make two piles: things that belong in your rucksack, and things that don't.

21 Put the things that don't belong in the rucksack where they do belong.

22 Put the things that do belong in your rucksack back, but in an organized way.

BE SMART

Here are some hints to help you organize your rucksack:

- Most rucksacks have several sections. Use them! An outside pocket is a great place for a water bottle. Put small items such as keys and pens in a small inside pocket so they don't get lost. Save the big compartment for big things such as books and clothes.
- Once you've decided where things should go, always put them back in the right compartment.
- Now that your backpack is a lean, mean, transporting machine, keep it that way. Go through it every week and take out anything you don't need.

Big stuff in the big compartment (because that's where it fits)

Lunch on top of big stuff (so it won't get squished)

Small things in small compartments (so you can find them)

Water bottle in an outer pocket (for easy access and so it won't flood your homework if it leaks)

Organizing your lesson notes

23 Colour-code your lessons. Choose a different coloured folder or binder for each lesson – for example, use red for history (because of all the bloody battles). You can even use ink in the same colours to record assignment due dates on your calendar.

24 Divide ring binders into different sections with tabs. (If you use spiral notebooks, you can make your own tabs out of tape.) You might have one section for lesson notes, one for assignments, and one for handouts.

25 Use binder pouches. Is there a piece of equipment you use for only one of your classes? For example, you might use your compass only for maths classes. Keep it in a zipped pouch, and pop the pouch in the maths class binder.

26 Leave notes at home if you don't need them for lessons. They'll be there when you need to study for your final exam. And if your backpack gets lost or stolen by enemy agents (or if you leave it on the bus – less exciting but more likely), you won't lose a whole term's worth of work.

BE SMART

Three ways to organize your notes

- If you don't have lots of paper to deal with, you might only need one ring binder for all your subjects. Use tabs to divide it into sections for each subject.
- Spiral notebooks work well for some people. On the plus side, the pages stay put. On the other hand, you can't reorder pages without ripping them out. Look for notepads with pockets so you'll have a place to put loose sheets of paper.
- Some people like keeping a different binder for each class. Use tabs to divide them into different sections. For example, your math binder might have tabs for class notes, assignments, handouts, and returned tests.

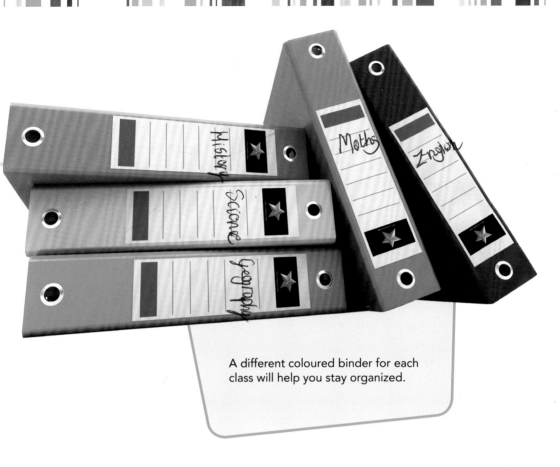

A different coloured binder for each class will help you stay organized.

BE SMART

Keep your computer files organized, too!

- Make a folder to hold all your schoolwork, especially if you share a computer. You can divide it into separate sub-folders for each lesson.
- When you make a file, take time to give it a name you'll remember later.
- Are you saving separate drafts of an essay? Put the date of each draft in the file name. That way you'll know which is the most recent.
- Super-important computer tip: back up critical files in case your computer crashes. No excuses – just do it!

27 Do you have trouble listening and taking notes at the same time? Ask your teacher if you can make a recording of your class.

28 Use abbreviations when you're taking notes. If there's a long word that keeps coming up, jot an abbreviation at the top of your note page, then use it. It's a lot quicker to write "Sh" instead of "Shakespeare", or "Ln" instead of "London".

29 If you have a lot to memorize, such as foreign words in a language lesson, keep going over things you've already learned. If you don't keep going back to them, they'll fade faster than a reality television star's fame.

BE SMART

Smart studying

Perhaps normal note-taking doesn't work for you? Try organizing your thoughts with a mind map. Start with the topic in the centre. Draw lines branching out from the centre for key points related to the topic. Then draw more lines branching from the key points for points related to them. Draw pictures and use different colours to make your map easier for you to understand. This works not just for studying, but also for things like packing for a holiday or planning a party.

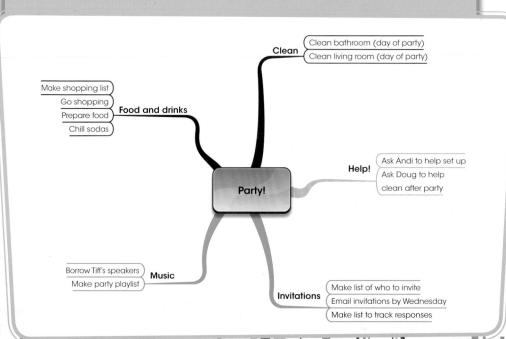

Clean
- Clean bathroom (day of party)
- Clean living room (day of party)

Food and drinks
- Make shopping list
- Go shopping
- Prepare food
- Chill sodas

Help!
- Ask Andi to help set up
- Ask Doug to help
- clean after party

Party!

Music
- Borrow Tiff's speakers
- Make party playlist

Invitations
- Make list of who to invite
- Email invitations by Wednesday
- Make list to track responses

Q

Help! I have a terrible memory – and a big test coming up!

A

Try using **mnemonic** devices to help you remember things. Here are some examples:

- The seven colours of the rainbow appear in this order: red, orange, yellow, green, blue, indigo, violet. Take the first letters of these words, put them together, and you get the anagram "Roy G. Biv." If you remember the pretend person Roy G. Biv, you'll have a very real way to get the rainbow order right.

- **M**rs **Nerg** can help you remember the seven life processes for your biology class: **m**ovement, **r**eproduction, **s**ensitivity, **n**utrition, **e**xcretion, **r**espiration, **g**rowth.

- *"Thirty days hath September,*
  April, June, and November;
  All the rest have thirty-one,
  Save February, with twenty-eight days clear,
  And twenty-nine each leap year."

- Make up a song to help you memorize groups of things. Setting things to music helps information stick in your brain.

When you're taking notes, using abbreviations can save you time (and pencil lead).

What's that?
A **mnemonic** is a device like a word or a rhyme that helps you remember something.

Organize your clothes

Clothes! You definitely need them. You may even love them. Whether you're a fashion victim or a jeans-and-trainers person, having your clothes in order will make getting dressed in the morning easier.

The first step in organizing your clothes is to get rid of any that you don't want or need. Then you can work out the best way to store what's left.

What's going on now?

What do your clothes storage areas look like? Can you find your clothes easily? Are your wardrobe and drawers stuffed with things that don't fit or need mending? What's working? What isn't?

If your wardrobe looks like this, fear not! Organizing it is probably easier than you think.

Costume craziness

Do you think organizing your clothes is difficult? It's a good thing you don't work at Angels The Costumiers in London. This company has about 5 million items on nearly 13 kilometres (8 miles) of racks! Some items are stored in separate sections. For instance, there's a wig department, a military department, and a shoe department. Other items are arranged by historical period. Within each period, they're divided into male and female items.

Getting rid of clothes and shoes you don't need is the first step towards a more organized wardrobe.

How to control your wardrobe

If it looks like a tornado's torn through your wardrobe, it's time to tame your clothing chaos. Follow these steps and you'll be sorted in no time.

- Pick some great music that will inspire you. Music will make the time fly.
- Line up three big bags or containers. Use one for clothes to be thrown out, one for clothes to give to a charity shop or swap with friends, and one for clothes that need mending.
- Take everything out of your wardrobe. Put it somewhere you can sort it, such as your bed.
- Start sorting. Be ruthless! Dump your collection of odd socks, clothes that can't be mended, and clothes that are badly worn out.
- Put clothes that you don't wear any more in the charity bag. (Check with an adult before throwing out or donating clothes to charity.)
- Pull out items that need to be mended. Promise yourself that they will not go back into your wardrobe until they're fixed!

If in doubt, throw it out! Better yet, give away the things you don't want to people who may need them more than you do.

Using your space efficiently means you can fit in much more than you thought possible.

- Try to use your space efficiently. If you need more hanging space, a double hanging rail can help. This hangs from the existing rail and doubles your hanging space. If you don't need to hang much, it might make sense to put your chest of drawers inside your wardrobe.
- Put everything away according to your new plan.

 Q I have too many clothes, but I have trouble letting anything go. What can I do?

 A Sometimes it helps to think about the people who really need clothes. Your too-small jacket can sit unworn in your wardrobe OR keep a homeless person warm. Which sounds better to you? If you still can't decide about some clothes, put them in a closed box for a year. If you don't miss them, it's probably safe to give them away.

More clothes know-how

30 Store things you wear all the time in places that are easy to get to. Put the stuff you don't wear very much on the high shelves in your wardrobe.

31 If you do store things on high shelves, keep a sturdy step-stool handy. Using your exercise ball or a flimsy cardboard box as a step-stool may seem like a brilliant idea when you're trying to get at something quickly. Trust us – it isn't!

Make sure you stay safe when you are reaching for things on high shelves.

32 Be creative when organizing your accessories. An interesting tree branch can be spray-painted and turned into a cool necklace holder.

33 Store your out-of-season clothes. Winter coats, scarves, and heavy jumpers can be bagged up and stored in the basement or attic during the summer. Summer shorts and beachwear can be stored during the winter.

This is not a good storage solution!

34 Keep nice shoes you don't wear often in boxes to keep them dust-free. You can buy plastic boxes for this. Or just use the box the shoes came in. Take a photo of the shoes and stick it on the outside of the box so you'll know at a glance which pair is inside.

35 Short on cupboard space? Fold jeans instead of hanging them up. Short on drawer space? Hang those jeans up!

36 Keep drawers tidy with organizers that divide up your drawer space.

37 Use clear boxes to organize belts, purses, and other small accessories. You'll always be able to see what's inside.

38 Have a clothes-exchange party with friends. Something you no longer wear might look fantastic on one of your mates!

39 Banish the crammed-cupboard blues: have a "one-thing-in, one-thing-out" rule. When you buy a new piece of clothing, get rid of one of your old ones.

listen up!

Move the clothes you plan to throw away or give to charity out of your room immediately. If you can't drop them off straight away, ask if you can put the bag in the car boot or garage. You don't need bags of clothes cluttering up your newly-organized room – and if they're sitting around, you might be tempted to dig around in the bag and rescue things you really don't want or need.

Organize your activities and social life

Sports and other activities are great as long as you don't try to do too many of them.

Singing, skateboarding, and rock-climbing are excellent hobbies, so why not do all of them? No reason – unless your activities start taking over your life.

It's great to have lots of different interests, but if you try to pursue them all at once you may find you're totally overbooked. If you're racing from one thing to the next, it's easy to get stressed out – and hard to enjoy anything. And what's the point of doing these activities if they're not fun?

What's going on now?
Do you feel overwhelmed? Are you sometimes expected to be in two places at once? Are you truly enjoying all the activities you've chosen? Do your friends or family complain that they never see you?

40 Ask yourself why you're taking on a new activity. Are you joining the debating team because you love debating? Or is it because you have a crush on the debating team captain? Be honest with yourself, especially if your schedule is already full. Is there a way you can accomplish the same thing without overloading your schedule?

41 Use pockets of time between school and activities. If school ends at 3.00 p.m. but your dance class isn't until 4.30 p.m., you have a good window of time to get some of your homework out of the way.

42 If you can, rearrange your schedule to make it more efficient. Can you join an early-morning swimming class rather than the one that meets at 6.00 p.m.? Does it make sense to move your piano lesson to Monday so you'll have the weekend to practise?

listen up!

Do you always feel drowsy after lunch? Are you buzzy in the morning but pooped at night? Everyone has certain times during the day when they work best. When you're scheduling your day, save your most demanding tasks for your best times. Do things that don't need a lot of brainpower at the other times.

Smart scheduling

Do you want to take up guitar, bellydancing , or karate? Perhaps you want to join the student council? Great – but give yourself a reality check. Make sure you know how much time a new activity will *really* take before you sign up.

A one-hour lesson doesn't sound like a big deal. But what if it's a 30-minute bus ride to get there? What if the teacher expects you to practise for an hour every day? All of a sudden you're looking at a nine-hour commitment every week.

Your student council may only meet once a month. But members may be expected to spend time raising money or helping with events. Knowing what you're really getting into will help you make good choices.

If you sign up for music lessons, be sure to make time for practising, too.

43 When travelling to your activities, allow extra time in case there's heavy traffic or you miss a bus connection.

44 Keep bus or train schedules and maps in your backpack to avoid transit trauma.

45 Don't be the person on the bus who makes the driver and all the other passengers wait while you hunt for your money or bus pass in your bag and pockets. Keep them somewhere easy for you (but not a pickpocket) to get at.

46 Turn your bus or train ride into a homework opportunity. If you study for half an hour on the way home, that's half an hour less study time that evening.

Take advantage of your journey to school by reading or studying.

47 Combine activities to save time. Cycling to school = transportation + exercise!

48 If you're totally swamped, see if you can swap household chores with a sibling. (Then help your sibling when he or she has too much to do.)

On the road

Sometimes it can feel like a major operation just getting your lunchbox, your rucksack, and your body all out of the door at the same time. Imagine how organized band roadies have to be!

When a band is on tour, roadies move equipment and set up the stage. For example, U2's 360° tour has a massive stage that requires 37 trucks to move it. There are three stages in total. While the group is performing in one place, stage crew are busy dismantling the stage from their previous tour stop. Meanwhile, the third stage is being assembled for the next tour date. The tour requires about 200 trucks in total, and they all need to be properly packed. It makes getting you and your gear to school look like a piece of cake!

Tending friendships

Making time for your friends is super-important. But it can be hard to see your mates when you're overloaded with schoolwork, household chores, and other activities. Here are some tips to make things easier:

49 Combine friendships with school activities. If you and your best friend both sing in the school choir, you'll see each other during (and before and after) every rehearsal. If you have a group of friends in your history class, consider getting together to study once a week (but make sure you actually get some studying done!).

Studying with friends is a good way to combine homework time and social time.

50 Keep track of your friends' birthdays. Write them on your calendar, or put them on your computer or phone.

51 Make sure you have your friends' phone numbers stored somewhere other than your mobile phone. If you lose your phone, you don't want to lose all the numbers as well!

52 Keep a stash of emergency birthday cards and gifts in case one of your friends' birthdays sneaks up on you.

53 Balance old friends with new ones. It may be tempting to hang out only with your long-term friends. But getting to know new people makes life more interesting.

54 If you need to cancel a date with a friend, do it as soon as you know so that he or she can make other plans. If you can make it, be sure you're on time. No one likes to be kept waiting.

55 Learn to say "no". Lots of people have impossible schedules because they can't say no without feeling guilty. It's great to see your friends, but not if it means ignoring the homework that's due in tomorrow. If you can't hang out with your best buddies on one day, suggest another date so they know you do really want to see them.

What is the difference between an introvert and an extrovert?

People who recharge their batteries by spending time alone are called introverts. People who get energy from being around other people are called extroverts. Although some people are right in the middle, most tend one way or the other.

If you're an introvert, you're probably happier spending one-on-one time with a close friend than going to a party. You also need time alone, so be sure to include that in your schedule.

If you're an extrovert, you find being around lots of people energizing. Too much time alone studying drives you mad, so schedule in breaks with friends to stay happy and productive.

Organize your room

Your room is your space, perhaps the only space that's totally yours. It should be a place where you feel comfortable, and where you can easily find what you need. Remember, you can be creative *and* organized! When your friends come over, you want them to think your room is a reflection of your sparkling personality. You don't want them to wonder if there's actually a floor hiding under all your junk.

What's going on now?

Is your room basically neat, or are there piles of paper and clothes everywhere? What would you say your biggest organization problem is? Even if your room's a mess, is there one group of things that is well organized?

If your guitar sleeps in your bed with you, it might be time to tidy up!

"A place for everything and everything in its place."

Isabella Mary Beeton (1836-1864), author

Zone out!

A good way to handle your room is to divide it into zones, or areas, for each of your main activities. To get started, think of the main things you do in your room:

- sleep
- study
- get dressed

You might also add:

- play guitar
- play video games
- read
- paint

Next, draw a rough sketch of the floor plan of your room. Then divide your room into areas for each of your activities. (Check with your parents if this means moving your furniture around.) Your clothes chest of drawers should be in the "get dressed" zone. Your desk should be in - you guessed it - the "study" zone. When you have everything you need for one task in a single area, it's easier to get things done. It's also easier to put things away.

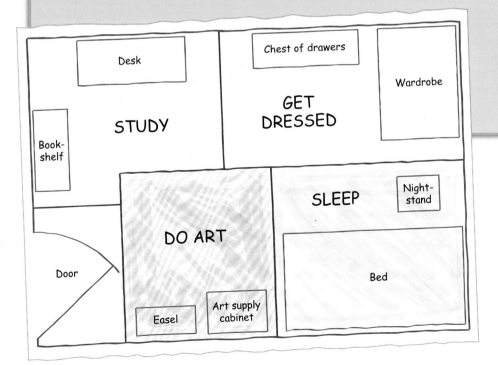

Ready ... steady ... CLEAN!

56 First things first: choose an after-cleaning reward! Looking forward to it will help keep you motivated.

57 If you've got lots of clutter, get rid of it (see helpful tips in previous chapters). This will make organizing what's left much easier.

58 Using the zone system, put everything where it belongs.

59 Once your room is fabulously organized, congratulations – it's reward time!

Plastic storage bins can help you get organized. Look for ones you can store under your bed.

Sometimes you want to hang on to something, not because you actually use it, but because of the memories it brings back. For instance, that gruesome pink and yellow statue you won at the fair might remind you of the fun you had that afternoon with your friends. To hang on to the memories, but lose the clutter, take a photograph of the item. When you look at the photo, the memories will come flooding back – but you won't have the statue falling on your head every time you open your cupboard.

case study

It pays to organize!

Whenever Richard came home, he dumped the contents of his pockets, including his money, in his room. Before he went to uni, his mum made him clean his room thoroughly. He ended up finding £32. Not bad for an afternoon's work!

Keep-it-tidy tips

60 Are missing pieces spoiling your board games? Make a checklist of everything that should be inside the box and glue it inside the box lid. That way you can make sure you've collected everything before you put the game away.

61 Yesss...! You landed those hot concert tickets! You definitely don't want to lose them. Keep a special place for important things like tickets and invitations. Attach them to a notice board – or clip them on your door at eye-level so you'll be sure not to forget them when you leave. You could also attach a notepad to your door and use it to write down things you need to remember.

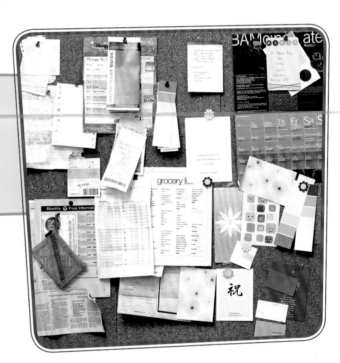

A notice board is a great place to keep tickets and other bits of paper that could get lost on your desk.

62 Okay, you wore the shirt for a few hours. It doesn't really need washing, but it's not sparkling clean either so you don't want to put it back in the drawer. "In between" clothes often end up draped over a chair or tossed into a corner. Create a special place or put up some hooks for "in-betweeners".

63 Choose organizing systems that work for you. Some people sort their book or CD collections into alphabetical order (author or title), into fiction or non-fiction titles, or into subjects (birds, music, history, or whatever). Find a system that you think makes sense.

64 Make your bed every day. This makes your room look neater instantly, and only takes a minute.

65 Once you've got your room in order, keep it organized with a quick daily pick-up of clutter. Just five minutes each evening should do the job.

You can find books in a library because there are systems in place to help you. Think like a librarian: organize your books alphabetically or by topic.

 I've got some bulky stuff in my room – what am I supposed to do with it?

 A bulky item can be a chore to store. Slide it under your bed to get it out of sight. Or think of it as cool decor, not a storage nightmare. For instance, hang a guitar holder on your wall to turn your instrument into art. Suspend your surfboard from the ceiling (ask your parents to help you with this).

If something is really huge and you don't use it that much, ask if you can store it in another part of your house, such as the basement or garage.

Organize your memories and collections

If your Bulgarian cereal box-top collection is so important to you, why is it sitting in a dusty box in the garage? What about all those photos stuck in the carrier bag in the back of your wardrobe, where they get crushed every time the horrible pink and orange statue you won at the fair falls on them? (Ahem, weren't you going to get rid of that?) They should be in a box or an album, not in a manky old bag.

Photos and souvenirs help you remember fun times. When you store them properly, you can really enjoy them. Collecting can be a rewarding hobby. Regardless of whether you collect railway tickets, coins, or tumble-dryer lint, you need a way to track and store new additions to your collection.

Coloured folders can help you organize souvenirs such as theatre programmes or fliers from gigs.

What's going on now?

Are your photos organized, or heaped in a bag under your bed? Are your souvenirs somewhere you can see and enjoy them, or in a mildewed box in the attic? Has your ever-growing stuffed animal collection turned your room into a zoo?

66 Newspaper cuttings decay quickly over time, and darken with exposure to light. If you want to save a super-important cutting (such as the newspaper photo of you backstage with your favourite band), search online for "preservation photocopying". This uses special machines to make more permanent copies.

67 Display birthday cards and postcards on a notice board in your room.

68 Do you collect ticket stubs or stray coins? Toss them into a cool box or a big jar.

69 Keep a diary. Sometimes words are the best way to preserve memories. Lots of famous authors start their days with a short diary-writing session.

There are advantages to storing your photos on your computer. You can share them easily, and you can keep them safe by backing them up.

"Set limits! Have one or two bins of mementos, photos, or games and that's it! Especially as you get older, it's important to re-evaluate what exactly is in those bins because what was important at age 6 is often not important at age 14."

Steven Franklin, professional organizer

Picture-perfect organization

There are lots of ways to organize your photos. Here's some help so you can decide which is best for you:

- If you like sharing photos with distant friends and relatives, a digital photo storage website is a good solution. You can invite others to your online album, and they can even buy prints.
- If you don't have internet access, you can store digital photos on your computer (but remember to back up!).
- If you'd rather have friends over to your house to look at photos, you might think about getting prints made and organizing them in photo albums.
- If you like doing crafts, scrapbooking might be for you. You can glam up your photos with decorations, stickers, and funny quotes.
- If you don't look at your photos very much, storing them in a box is an easy, no-fuss solution.

Scrapbooking tips

- Crop till you drop: crop photos to get rid of unneeded background. You can also cut them into fun shapes, such as hearts.
- Help with messy handwriting: use individual letter stickers or stamps to spell out words.
- No regrets: arrange the whole page before you start gluing things down.

70 Computers can store tonnes of photos in a tiny space, but if your computer breaks, your photos may be gone for good. Always remember to back up! Safeguard your memories by copying your photo files to a portable hard drive, which is generally more reliable than a CD. For extra protection, upload them to an online photo-sharing service. Or email the photos to relatives.

71 If a photo is blurry, or the person in the photo has closed eyes or a goofy expression, dump it or delete it. This is true for prints and digital photos. Digital photos take up storage space on your computer, and all those bad photos make it harder to find the good ones you actually want to look at.

72 Label photos with who is in them and the date and place they were taken. You may know now that the boy in the picture is Herbert, your neighbour's cousin, but there's no guarantee you'll remember that in 30 years' time.

73 Organize digital photos as soon as you load them on to your computer.

74 Choose a way to organize your photos that works for you. You can do this by date or by event. Some computer programs even help you sort them by person. Search online for tips about using the software you choose. Computer magazines at the public library may also have helpful articles.

75 Save space by using a digital photo frame to display lots of photos. Prefer printed photos? Hang a **collage** of photos in a frame on the wall.

Whether you prefer prints or digital photos, a good organizing system will help keep your memories at your fingertips.

Conquer your collections

76 If you're starting a collection, keep in mind how much space it will take up as your collection grows. Need space for a collection of stamps or charms? Pretty simple. Need space for a collection of six-foot-tall carved wooden bears or full-sized HGV tyres? Not so easy.

77 Use the right type of storage for your collection, especially if the items are valuable. If you type "how to store comic books" or "how to store vintage football cards" into an internet search engine, you'll find some good ideas for the things you collect.

> Some collectors store their comics in plastic bags... after they've read them, of course!

78 Keep track of what's in your collection. You can use a computer spreadsheet or database, or a notebook. When you add an item, record what it is, the date you got it, and the price you paid for it. An electronic spreadsheet will let you sort your collection by value, date of purchase, or who you bought things from.

79 Use a **floating shelf** to display collectibles.

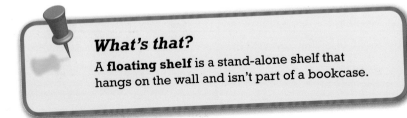

What's that?
A **floating shelf** is a stand-alone shelf that hangs on the wall and isn't part of a bookcase.

Whether you collect rocks or robots, learn how to store your collection properly.

80 A hammock hanging in the corner of a room will keep stuffed animals on display but out of the way.

81 Rethink your collecting habits once in a while. Just because you started collecting coins or dolls when you were younger doesn't mean you still enjoy it now. If collecting starts to feel like a chore it might be time to call it quits. You may want to keep what you've already collected, but just decide not to add to it. Or you might sell the items to make some extra cash. Another option: pass your collection on to someone who will enjoy it. It might make a wonderful birthday gift!

case study

Creative collecting

Collections don't have to be expensive, and they can be silly! Steve Silberberg collects something most people don't even want to think about: air-sickness bags from aeroplanes. He scans each bag, puts it into a database, and posts it on his website.

Steve started collecting in 1981 and now has over 2,000 bags from all over the world. He says that you should start collecting because you think it's fun, not because you hope your collection will be valuable one day. One more tip from Steve: "Don't collect anything you'll eventually need an extra room in your house for."

Organize your family

Even if you totally love your family, they may drive you mad sometimes. Does your brother or sister borrow your stuff without asking? Do your parents forget to sign permission slips and other forms from school?

There are ways to help your family understand what you need, and for them to help you understand what they need. As in all relationships, communication is crucial.

What's going on now?

When your family is going out somewhere, is everyone ready on time? Does each family member know which jobs he or she is responsible for? Are there rules about borrowing things from other family members?

Kids aren't the only ones with time-management problems. Parents lose track of time, too!

Need to be somewhere on time? Your family might appreciate a ten-minute warning.

82 If it's your job to do the washing up, do it immediately after the meal. You know you'll have to do it eventually. Don't make your parents ask you over and over again. It wastes their time, and puts everyone in a bad mood.

83 Calendars make good presents for people in your family (especially the ones who are always forgetting things).

84 Does your little brother hop in circles around you while you're trying to do your homework? Guess what, he probably just wants your attention. Instead of yelling at him, tell him you'll play with him for 10 minutes, but after that you have to do your homework.

85 If you've promised to help someone, or to do a chore by a certain time, do it. No excuses. Never promise something you can't do or people won't trust you the next time.

86 If your family has trouble getting out of the house in the morning, a clock in the breakfast area might help. Or run through the house yelling, "We need to leave in 10 minutes!" like a town crier from the olden days (the costume and bell are optional).

87 Now and again, try to say one nice thing to each person in your family. Just saying something like, "Dad, thanks for always being there to help me with my maths homework," is all it takes. (Note: the time to say this is when Dad isn't expecting it, not just before you ask him for some extra cash!)

88 Make a chore chart for your family so everyone's clear on which jobs to do. Things run more smoothly when everyone knows what's expected of them.

89 If there are too many people and not enough bathrooms, agree on a morning and evening rota for showers or baths. Stick the rota on the bathroom door.

90 You open your favourite cereal packet and there are three lonely flakes at the bottom of the box. Avoid the dreaded empty-packet crisis: put a magnetic shopping list on the fridge door.

91 If you need your parents or carers to sign a school form, don't fling it in their faces as you're running out of the door. Explain what it is, and give them time to look it over.

92 What's the one sentence all parents hate hearing? "Mum, I need a Godzilla outfit for the school play today!" If you need something from your parents, give them as much notice as you can.

93 Adults are busy too – help them to help you! If your dad is making the set for your school play, offer to help him paint the background.

94 A family calendar will help prevent schedule conflicts. Use a different coloured pen for each person so you can see at a glance who's doing what each day.

95 Did your mum promise to pick up your choir outfit from the cleaners? Call her, or send her a text message to remind her.

If your parents promise to run an errand for you, send a friendly text message to remind them.

96 If your parents aren't very mobile-phone-savvy, email reminders work too. So does sticking a note on the car windscreen!

97 Remember to say THANK YOU when someone helps you. For even more impact, write a thank-you card or get them a small gift.

Room-sharing problems? Try dividing the room down the centre!

 I share a room with my younger sister. HELP!

 Keeping your room organized is difficult enough without someone else helping to mess it up. You can try talking with your sister and explaining (nicely) why you want to keep the room clean and tidy. But she may not understand, or care. If that's the case, see if you can divide the room down the middle somehow. A row of bookcases might work. Or put a non-marking strip of tape down the centre!

Throw anything she leaves on your side of the room into a big box. If she leaves lots of things on your side, talk to your parents about another solution; for instance, if she leaves a toy on your side, she can't play with it the next day.

What if nothing works? Try not to let it get to you. If you end up with a slobby housemate at uni, you'll already have had years of experience coping with it!

Organize your time

No one ever seems to have enough time! Between school, family, friends, activities, and household chores, you may feel like you don't even have time to breathe, let alone relax. Don't worry! There are lots of tools to help you organize your time.

What's going on now?

Do your parents have to drag you out of bed each morning by your ankles to get you up? Do you feel like you're always rushing? Do you do your schoolwork at the very last minute?

You may find getting up can be a bit of a chore, but your parents probably feel the same if they have to nag you to get out of bed!

Procrastinating and wasting time go together like fish and chips. If you're avoiding doing your homework, you'll probably end up doing something useless (like playing solitaire on the computer) rather than something useful (like helping with the washing up). If you can zap procrastination, you'll be surprised at how much time you free up.

What's that?
If you **procrastinate**, it means that you put off doing tasks that you know you need to do.

Quiz

Are you a procrastinator?

1. You told your teacher you'd make some chocolate biscuits for the school fête today. When do you bake them?
   - a. I made them last night
   - b. I got up early to make them, but we're out of flour.
   - c. I totally overslept. Do you think these dog biscuits could pass for biscuits if I slap a little icing on them?

2. Your final history assignment was set in March and is due in June. How do you organize your time?
   - a. I made a schedule: the reading in March, outlining in April, first draft in May, and a final check the week before it's due
   - b. In May I'll dig out the assignment, then I'll work on the report for the two weeks before it's due
   - c. I'll just stay up late the night before it's due. Very late. Very, very late…

3. It's your turn to wash the car. When do you do it?
   - a. It's already done. It was on my calendar so I put it on my "to-do" list for today.
   - b. I'll do it after Dad reminds me.
   - c. I'll do it after I've messaged my best friend 10 times, and examined my feet to see if they're really the same size or if one's bigger, and tried to sing the alphabet song backwards in less than 15 seconds...

Find out the truth!

If your answers are:

Mostly a's: good work! You keep track of time and make the most of it.

Mostly b's: a few time-management tips could help you out.

Mostly c's: the people who would have answered mostly c's never got around to taking the test.

More time-saving tips

98 Make a checklist every evening of the things you need to do the next day. To make sure you don't lose the list, put it where you'll be sure to see it. Or stick it on that pink and orange statue. (HEY! Isn't that in the bin yet?!)

99 Lay out your clothes at night before you go to sleep.

Getting ready in the morning is easier if you don't have to decide what to wear.

100 Do you sleep through your alarm clock? Put it across the room from your bed, so you'll have to get up to turn it off. You can also set your mobile phone alarm or MP3 player alarm as a back-up.

101 Regular five-minute stretches or walks will help keep up your levels of concentration. Take short breaks while you study and you'll actually get more done.

102 Don't **multitask**. It's more efficient to do one thing at a time rather than switching back and forth (between email, homework, and texting your friends, for instance).

What's that?
Multitasking means doing more than one thing at once.

Feeling pressed for time? Before you start dropping activities you enjoy, take a look at where your time really goes. Keep a time log for a day. Set up a computer spreadsheet, or just use a notebook. For example, your entries might look like this:

- 7.30–7.45 a.m. – showered and got dressed
- 7.45–8.05 a.m. – ate breakfast
- 8.05–8.10 a.m. – got school stuff together

Be honest! At the end of the day, look at how you spent your time. Any surprises? If you feel too busy but you spent four hours playing games on your phone, you might want to rethink your priorities.

"The mobile phone has a lot of features, but most of them aren't used. The alarm feature not only can wake us up in the morning, it can provide reminders throughout the day. For example, set it to remind you to study for an exam. Use the voicemail service to send yourself reminder messages."

Geralin Thomas, professional organizer

Q How much time do we waste?

A It varies from person to person, but according to one study, many young people watch at least three hours of television each day. That's more than one sixth of your waking life!

103 *Over*estimate the time needed for each task on your "to-do" list. That way you won't be thrown off schedule if you hit a snag. If you do get something done earlier than expected, you'll feel good!

104 Do unpleasant tasks first. It's better just to do them than to have them hanging over your head all evening.

105 Procrastinating? Getting started is often the hardest part of a job. Set a timer for ten minutes, and tell yourself you can stop after that. Once you get started, you often find it's not as bad as you thought, so you keep going!

Oops!

The internet is a great source of information, but it's easy to get sucked into spending lots of time aimlessly browsing. There's actually a computer program that blocks a computer's internet access for a certain length of time. That way the user can get some work done! (Adults waste even more time online than kids do!)

listen up!

Exam tomorrow? Big audition coming up? Here's a quick guide to tackle stress:

- Set a kitchen timer or the timer on your phone for five minutes. Sit comfortably and close your eyes.

- Inhale slowly. Concentrate on the air coming in through your nose and down into your lungs.

- Hold your breath for a few seconds, then slowly exhale. Pay attention to the flowing air.

- As you continue to breathe slowly, imagine that you're in one of your favourite places. It might be a forest, a tropical island, or even a place you've made up. Focus on your surroundings – palm trees, streams, mountains. Continue to breathe slowly and imagine until the timer rings.

106 Make a new habit. If you have a daily commitment (for instance, practising piano), try doing it at the same time each day.

Writing things down can help you remember them. Or use the memo function on your phone.

BE SMART

Choose the right calendar for you

The more activities you do, the more you need a calendar – the *right* calendar.

If you like writing things down, choose a paper calendar. A desk calendar that you leave at home works if you're not running around a lot. Or choose a nice one that looks great on your wall. If you're on the go all the time, get a calendar you can carry with you.

If you're a computer wizard, use your computer's calendar function. Or use an online calendar that will let everyone in your family see one another's schedules. Synchronize either with your phone or MP3 player so you can check your schedule while you're out.

Glossary

collage form of art where photos, drawings, or pieces of fabric are arranged and stuck on to a piece of cardboard or other backing

floating shelf shelf that hangs on the wall and is not part of a bookcase

mnemonic something that acts as a memory aid

multitask do more than one thing at once

procrastinate put off doing something that needs to be done

Oops!

Even the most organized people have bad days. If you've lost something, follow these steps:

1. Take a few deep breaths. It has to be somewhere.
2. Close your eyes and think of where you saw it last.
3. If that doesn't help, retrace your steps. Where were you when you last had it? What did you do immediately after that? Keep your eyes peeled.
4. Follow any hunches. If you have a weird feeling that your watch is in the boot of the car, it could be your subconscious trying to help you.
5. Think about what was happening when the item was lost. Did you mean to put your wallet in your rucksack and your leftover pasta in the fridge? If you got distracted, you might have accidentally put your wallet in the fridge. (If you were really distracted, you might have put the pasta in your rucksack.)

Quiz

Are you a wardrobe wizard or a clothes catastrophe?

Do you have any clothes that you don't wear?
- a. No. I washed them all and gave them to charity.
- b. Yes. I'm keeping some T-shirts for sentimental reasons.
- c. Yes. I've got tonnes of clothes. I'm hanging on to them in case I ever need them.

When you open your wardrobe door, what happens?
- a. Nothing
- b. A shirt falls out occasionally
- c. Avalanche!

What's your shoe situation?
- a. My shoes are organized on a shoe rack so I can always find them.
- b. They're piled on the floor of my wardrobe. If I dig around long enough, I can usually find the ones I want.
- c. Hey – I wear different shoes on each foot because it's a fashion statement. It's definitely not because I can't find the other one…

What do you keep in your middle drawer?
- a. That's where my socks and T-shirts go: socks on the left, t-shirts on the right.
- b. I think some of my jumpers are there, along with a clay dinosaur I made when I was six.
- c. I don't know – it's so crammed full of stuff that it's been stuck shut for months. Do you have a crowbar I can borrow?

Find out the truth!

If your answers are:

Mostly a's: congratulations! You're a clothes genius!

Mostly b's: a little clothing know-how wouldn't hurt you.

Mostly c's: you need to get organized fast – before you get swallowed up by a mountain of laundry!

Find out more

Books

Life Skills: Managing Money, Barbara Hollander (Raintree, 2009)

Life Skills: Study for Success, Tessa Phipps (Raintree, 2009)

The Clutter Clinic: Organise Your Home in Seven Days, Romaine Lowery (Weidenfeld & Nicolson, 2008)

The Indispensable Book of Practical Life Skills, Nic Compton (New Holland Publishers, 2009)

The Seven Habits of Highly Effective Teenagers, Sean Covey (Simon & Schuster, 2004)

Time Management for Dummies, Clare Evans (John Wiley & Sons, 2008)

Websites

www.guardian.co.uk/lifeandstyle/2010/jul/16/teenagers-bedrooms
Read about how these young people organize their bedrooms.

www.humanities.manchester.ac.uk/studyskills/organising/time_management/how_to_organise.html
Visit this website for some great ideas on how to organise your time.

www.bbc.co.uk/webwise/guides/organising-emails
Use the handy tips you'll find on this website to organize your email inbox.

www.oxfam.org.uk/donate/shops/index.html
The website of the charity Oxfam gives advice on which of your unwanted items you can donate to them.

www.barnardos.org.uk/donate/donating_goods.htm
Barnardos is a charity dedicated to helping children in need. Visit their website to find out what items you can donate to help them raise money.

Index